Once Upon a Starry Night

The Story of Baby Jesus

Long ago, in a humble stable, under shining stars, a beautiful story of a baby with a big purpose began. Let's discover the story of Baby Jesus!

A long time ago, in a town called Nazareth,
there lived a kind woman named Mary.

One day, an angel named Gabriel visited Mary.
The angel told her that she would have a
special baby, and she should name him Jesus.

Mary was going to marry a man named Joseph. He was surprised about the baby, but an angel in his dream told him that everything would be okay.

Before Baby Jesus was born, Mary and Joseph had to take a long trip to a town called Bethlehem.

They traveled for many days through the
hot desert and saw many palm trees.

When Mary and Joseph got to Bethlehem, there were so many people that all the inns were full!

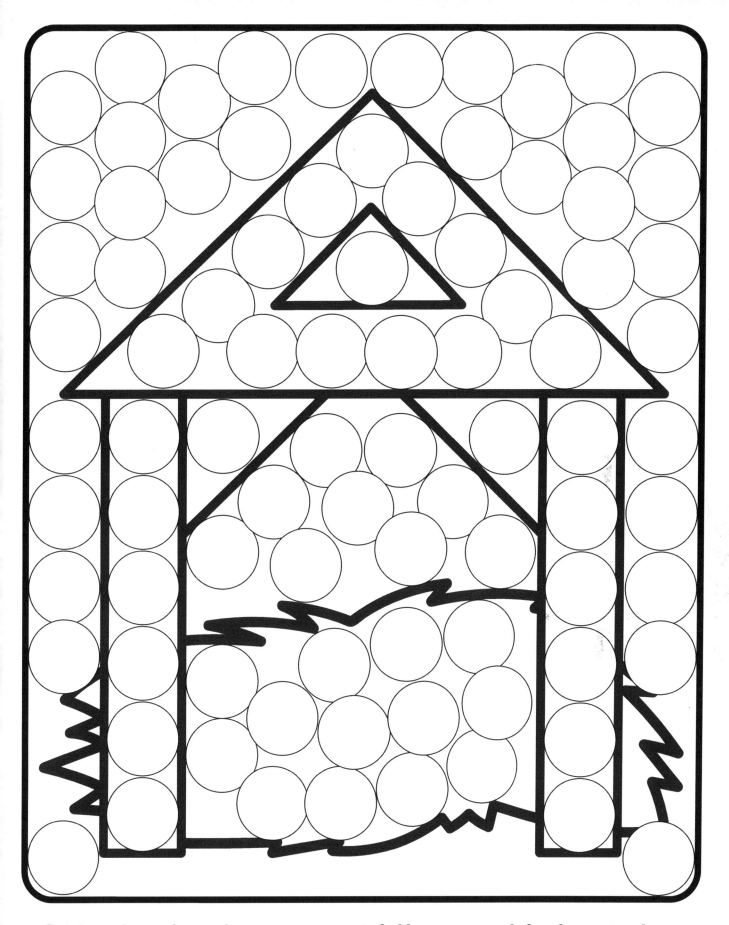

But a kind innkeeper said they could stay in his
stable where the animals slept.

That night, in the cozy stable, Baby Jesus was born. Mary wrapped him in soft clothes and laid him in a manger, which is like a bed for animals to eat from.

The cow in the stable gazed gently at Baby Jesus, watching over the special family with big, kind eyes.

In the fields nearby shepherds were
watching their sheep in the dark night.

Suddenly, the sky lit up with angels singing and celebrating the birth of Jesus.

The angels told the shepherds and sheep about the special baby, and they hurried to see Him.

Far away from the stable, three wise kings
saw a bright star in the sky.

**The kings knew the star meant a
special king was born.**

They followed the star all the way to Bethlehem.

The three Kings traveled on camels across the lands to visit Baby Jesus in the stable.

When they arrived, they saw a radiant light
shining around Baby Jesus, with Mary and Joseph
lovingly watching over him.

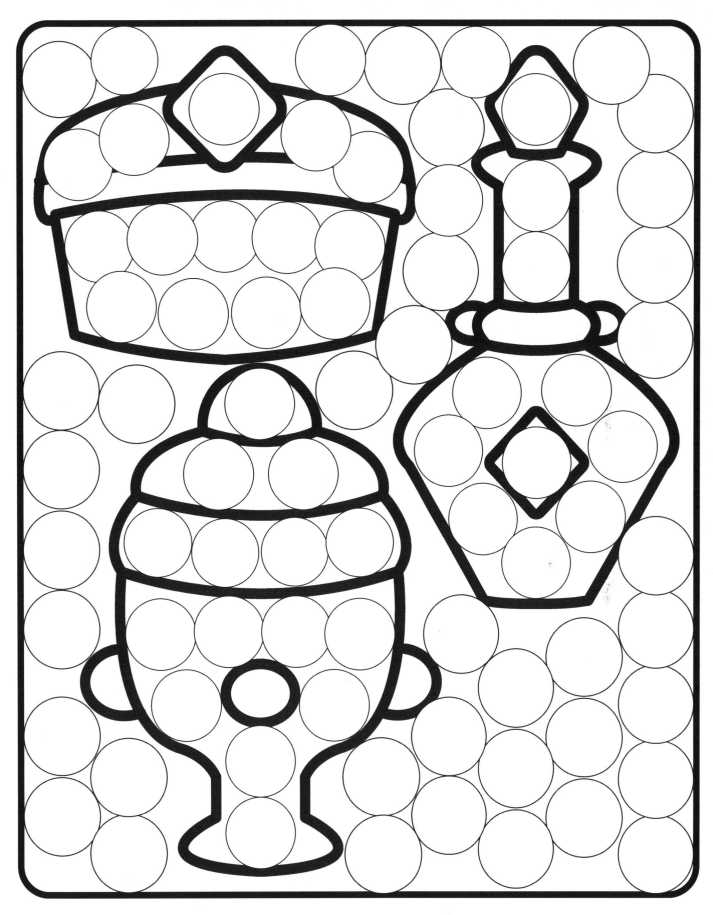

The three kings presented their special gifts for
Baby Jesus: gold, frankincense, and myrrh.

The shepherds who had kept watch over the stable
went to spread the news about Baby Jesus.

They left and spread the Good Word across
the land. Our Messiah had been born!

Everyone was so happy and thankful. They knew that Baby Jesus was a gift from God.

They would always remember how much God
loved them, and every night, they would say
a little prayer to thank Him.

The love and kindness that Baby Jesus brought
didn't stay just in that stable. It spread everywhere,
like the sun's rays on a bright morning!

Just like the shepherds and the wise kings,
we can share the love of Jesus by being
kind to everyone we meet.

Did you like coloring and learning about the birth of Jesus? This story and many other amazing stories are all found in the Bible!

My name is:

_____

I promise to say Thank You to Jesus and God for all the love they give us.

I promise to be kind, just like Jesus wants us to be.

When we're kind, the world becomes a brighter and happier place for everyone!

Made in United States
Orlando, FL
24 November 2024